When Did You Find Out?

2

When Did You Find Out?

X. Allen Sr.

J. Garrett

J.A. Eberhard

2021 Allen Wright Inc.

BURIED MINDZ

Instagram: _wdyfo

Facebook: When Did You Find Out?

Table Contents

Baby Boomer's: 1945 - The Early 1960s

Eberhard

Delaney

Johnnie

Martin

Darryl

Generation X: Late 1960's – 1970's

Garrett

Frost

Ray

Allen Sr.

Generation Y: The 1980's-1990's

Author Michael Gerald Hyland

Generation Z: (Millennial): Late 1990's-2000s

A. Isaiah

Dedication

This publication of *When Did You Find Out* humbly identifies and holds the human beings who took the time to unveil the intimate stories of their true encounters of self-awareness. Each one of the contributors willingly made amends and by doing this, is able to be a part of the betterment of humanity. Acknowledging this is important, because this is where all the transparencies lie. With this exposure brings forth each contributor's brutal deep seeded truth. At some point in each of their lives, the deception of this thing called 'RACE', was instilled in their psyche. Albeit, in an unbeknownst way to each one of them, yet the revelation is a testament to this offering.

The introduction to race and the discrimination that followed infiltrated their train of thought, with unbridled awareness. In the end, each contributor used vulnerabilities to assist with breaking through the barriers of the misguided information that each one of them had been continuously subjected to.

As each of the contributors had to come to realization, we ask you the reader the question, "When did you find out?"

PREFACE

What's the difference between a fisherman fishing in murky water or clear water? The transparency.

We present this question referencing the conditions of the water, murky or clear, as truth and lies. The murky water masquerades as truth, which is how this deep seeded lie of race is being presented to the world. This murky water has been concealed from the world. This concealment has caused a fundamental indifference that's constantly being regurgitated in the consciousness of mankind and must be eradicated at once.

 As a noun, race is defined as a group of sentients (a conscious life form capable to feel sensation) beings, distinguished by common heritage (a tradition) of characteristics. By way of ignorance, the concept of 'RACE' is misrepresented from its true definition.

In order to give clear recognition to our true value, let's identify the factual meaning of the human race. Below are the comprehensive and relatable terms:

- Mankind- the human race in its entirety.
- Humanity-is the human being. Identified as a group; their condition or nature, and the qualities of having a disposition to do well.
- Homo sapiens any of a species of biped (a being that goes about on two feet, or two legs).

The above definitions comprise all living persons and their recent ancestors. With the previous academic understanding, our human 'Ancestor' didn't classify 'Race' according to pigmentation, like our modern nations.

According to sociologist James M. Henslin, author of *A Down To Earth Approach,* "Sociologists Stress that what we call 'Race' are social classifications, not biological categories. Furthermore, sociologists point out that our 'Race' depends more on the society in which we live than on our biological characteristics."

The ancient people identified 'Race' in relation to one's national or tribal names such as: Ethiopian, Visigoths, Persians, Moors, Canaanites, Amalekites, Turkish, Slavic, and Cushites, etc.

The ways in which race was determined were changed after the renaissance period (1400-1600). During this period, the world was divided in reference to the coloration of human beings. Anthropologist Johann F. Blumenbach (1752-1840) was the first to divide humanity based on skin color. His study was rooted in 'Ethnography' a branch of Anthropology that scientifically describes specific human cultures, and societies. Blumenbach went on to classified 'FIVE' chief races of mankind:

- The Caucasian
- The Malayan
- The Mongolian
- The Ethiopian
- The American

This 'caste system' attributed psychological

disadvantages where, the defining of oneself with the misconception of 'race' was based on pigmentation instead of tribal, or cultural background. Henson was very vocal about this in his writings. He wrote,

"A caste system status is determined by birth and is lifelong. Someone born into a low-status group will always have low status, no matter how much that person may accomplish in LIFE. In sociological terms, the basis of a Caste System is ascribed status. Achieved status cannot change an individual's place in this system."

What Henslin was referring to is also created 'Pigmentocracy'. Which is government by or social hierarchy to those within a skin color, regardless of race or socioeconomic status.

Foot note:

Ethnos: a Greek word meaning people or nation, in the sense of classification of human beings.

Hierarchy: Root word-hierarch: one who possess the highest title to obedience and honor: and is the controlling Authority.

According to Anthropologist Ashley Montagu, author of *The Concept of Face, New York: Free Press,* and *Race and IQ: Expanded Edition,* "Large groupings of people can be classified by blood type and gene frequencies, even these classifications do not uncover 'Face'. Rather they are so arbitrary that biologists and anthropologists cannot even agree on how many races there are."

This cultural looting has polluted our chance of social advancement beyond the manufactured ignorance of 'Race'. It also refers to the historical background of the human being's identity, and cultural patrimony, being pillaged of its opportunity concerning cultural harmony. These unfavorable circumstances have established and tapped into our human nature to be competitive with those who are genetically different. Thus, willing to create opponents for financial gratification.

In conclusion this self –awareness is completely invested in one's inalienable right to be reunited with the true essence of "our being". Martin Luther King JR. once stated; "No lie can live forever." Which brings us to the question: "When did you find out", you were required to identify with a pre-prescribed **RACE.**

Etymological Research

For a more thorough understanding, this is the ETYMOLOGICAL RESEARCH:

These are the suffixes placed at the end of national or tribal names. They enhance the terminologies of our social systematic form of observation (empirical). They acknowledge customs, habits, beliefs, values, and behaviors related to cultural identification.

Ian: Adj-form, related to, or like; noun-one from, belonging to.

Ic: Used to form an adjective from a noun = characteristic

Or, pertaining to; often added to words of Greek or Latin origin.

Ish: of a nationality, region, or place; or the language associated with a place.

Ite: Refers to a descendant, native, or resident of a specified place or historical person.

Patrimony: A right or estate inherited from one's father or in a larger sense-from any ancestor.

The Chapter's Epitome

Our (American) generations: Baby Boomers, Generation X, Generation Y, and Generation Z (millennials); have produced a unique set of social circumstances in relation to ideas, beliefs, presumptions, and interpretations. These short stories are categorized to acknowledge and expose the true essence of self. It also identifies the damage 'Pigmentocracy' has evolved into.

Baby Boomers

1945-Early 1960's

<u>Important Political Events:</u>

1948: Kinsey report on sexuality in the human male is published

1949: President Truman on October 26, signed legislation raising the Federal minimum wage from 40 cents an hour to 75 cents.

1957: Brown v. Board of Educatio : May 17

1957: Congress approved Civil Rights Act April 29

1959: Alaska admitted as the 49th state: January 3, Hawaii admitted as 50th State August 21.

1960: President Eisenhower signed Civil Rights Act May 6.

1963: Gideon v. Wainwright, March 18th. Supreme Court

Ruled all criminal defendants must have counsel.

Sports:

Batting Champion Stan Musial: 1946, 1948, 1950, 1951, 1952, and 1957.

Jackie Robinson enters Baseball: April 11, 1947.

Betsy Rawls-Women's U.S. Open: 1951, 1953, 1957, 1960.

Althea Gibson- Wimbledon Champion: 1957, 1958

Roger Bannister, Track and Field-time: Broke the four-minute mile: 1958.

Willie Mays Major League Baseball National League Home Runs 1955 with 51, 1956 with 49, 1964 with 47.

Mickey Mantle Major League Baseball, American League Home Runs 1955 with 37, 1957 with 52, 1958 with 42, and 1960 with 40

Cassius Clay (Muhammad Ali), KO's Sonny Liston 1964-February 25.

Household Names:

Martin Luther King, Jr.

Frank Lucas

Rat pack: Joey Bishop, Frank Sinatra, Jerry Lewis, Sammy Davis Jr. and Dean Martin.

Popular Music:

Founder of Rock & Roll: Little Richard

King of Rock & Roll: Elvis Presley

King of Funk: James Brown

Do-Wop: Franky Valli and the Four Seasons

Folk Music: Carter Family (Country Music)

R & B: Muddy Waters

Jazz: Big Band

<u>Popular Television Shows or Movies:</u>

Movies: Gone with The Wind, To Kill A Mocking Bird, Ben Hur.

Television Shows: The Ed Sullivan Show, The Lone Ranger & Tonto, The Little Rascals, Abbot & Costello, Three Stooges, Gun Smoke, and The Lucy Show.

<u>World Events</u>

United States drops atomic bomb on Hiroshima, Japan. August 6th, Nagasaki, Japan, August 9th. Japan agreed to surrender on August 14, 1945.

North Korea invaded South Korea on June 25, 1950: Creating the Korean War

The Korean War (1) Armistice signed July 27, 1953.

March on Washington D.C.-Martin Luther King Jr. – I Have a Dream speech 1963.

President John F Kennedy killed on November 22, 1963 in downtown Dallas, TX.

Vietnam War begins in February 12, 1955.

Foot Note:

Armistice: a formal agreement to end fighting.

18

Martin Luther King found out he was black when he went to school with his friend who was white, and they wasn't able to play together

John A. Eberhard

56 years old born November 19, 1964

Sioux Falls, South Dakota

Raised in Sioux City, Iowa

Plymouth County

Mother: Margret Wright

Irish born 1936

Father: Norman Eberhard

Born Irish Name: Martin Newnan

Adopted by German farmer Walter and Rose Eberhard in 1933

(Iowa)

I'm John A, Eberhard the sixth child of seven kids. Four girls and three boys six and a half years age difference from the oldest to the youngest. I was born in 1964, my siblings and I were a very tight knit group, a typical Irish Catholic family or so it seemed.

Fast forward a few years to 1969. I was four and a half years old, and my father was sentenced to a two-year prison term for writing a bad check to Sears, Roebuck & Company. What's interesting is that my siblings and I weren't told until we were in our late 30's and early 40's. I guess it was a well-kept secret.

My mother, although a very strong and devoted woman, was not financially equipped to care for seven children under eleven years old. To feed, clothe, and put a roof over our heads. Soon after my father's incarceration all seven of us were placed in a county home facility for children in Sioux Falls, South Dakota. This place was huge to a child's eye, like an old-fashioned sanitarium.

Brutal staff conditions with no love given, except for my siblings contact when that was allowed, doing play time, was what I became accustomed to. It was the only love and nurturing I received. My sister and I were so small and young that we were placed in the pediatrics wards for children under the age of five years old. We later discovered that the ward was really meant for the children that were adoptable faster than the older kids.

Out of all my siblings, I was fortunate enough to be taken home by a young lady that was a schoolteacher. I remember her giving me a Captain Kangaroo pull tab speaking doll. After I was placed in a family home setting, my grandparents stepped in and made sure all of my siblings and I would not be split up. Their intervention was the catalyst of my parents getting their selves together. That led to a normal family structure or so we thought.

We moved to a farm we called Kulp's Place which was the original farmer who owned the property some fifty years before we got it. I think my parents paid fifth dollars a month for it and that was a task even then. We were a couple of years older now and my brothers Norm Jr., Joe, my two sisters and I enjoyed living on the farm a little bit. We often played Cowboys and Indians.

Norm was the oldest, so he called the shots. By his decision I was told that I was now an Indian native, with red skin. Indians, or as my brothers would say, "fucking Indians". So, we played as children do but this time it was different. I was seven years old faster and could hide really good but norm caught me and I thought the game was over as usual.

We played our favorite pastime often, but one day stood out from memory the best. One day, the game had taken a different route. I was now a savage enemy in my brother Norm's eyes and not his brother. I was the Indian that had to be killed. Doing this particular playtime, I realized I didn't want to be a Indian, because they had to be killed. In this was the moment I realized I didn't want to be an Indian.

Norm placed me in a chair with a rope or "hang man's noose" as he called it around my neck. The rope was attached to the top of the clothesline pole on the side of the house. I remember saying, "I don't want to be an Indian anymore, I want to be a cowboy.

Norm just simply stated, "you're an Indian and you must die you savage."

He then kicked the chair out from under me, and my reality changed in that second, I was to be the dead Indian (injun) as he called it. I grabbed the rope and struggled with my feet dangling three feet off the ground. Luckily, my sister came to my aid wrapped her little arms around my legs and lifted me up.

My brother was pissed. He said let the Indian hang awhile. After I was freed, I was rushed to the hospital by car with a serve rope burn around my neck. Dr. Walpert, my eyes, ears, nose, and throat doctor as they were called, said I would have died instantly if my hands would have been tied behind my back.

The doctor told my mother not to punish my brother for this because it would do a different kind of damage, an emotional one, to all of us. Well, she didn't listen and whooped the shit out of Norm. She was so pissed that I almost died. Her anger had nothing to do with the fact of the game we were playing. She didn't tell us why Cowboys killed Indians.

My brother already knew what I had just found out; differences in skin make a difference. The white cowboy was more powerful than the Indian. On that one Saturday afternoon on a farm in Iowa, something had been instilled in me because of that event.

 I'm now 55 years old and I've been a diehard Kansas City Chiefs fan for over 50 years. Which I didn't know or even realize for some 35 plus years later was the reason my brother made me the Indian that day; it was because I was a Chiefs fan. And he hated the Chiefs. But what was most important, was my new awareness of people being different because of their skin. This revelation almost took the life of an innocent child through the eye of another child's way of seeing skin and the hatred that comes from difference. It changed me and everyone in my family forever!

Delaney Franklin, C-90255

DOB: 1964

V.S.P D2-10-4L

P.O Box 92

Chowchilla, CA 93610

Date: June 24, 2020

Sub: When I Found Out I Was Black

Black is a color and not a state of mind of one's true heritage, because there's no place in the world called Blackland. I am African American because I am descendant of that bloodline. Looking back in hindsight there is no great defining moment of true clarity that I can speak on, that taught me about being African American. My revelation was a continuous process of mental evolution that brings about a consciousness of self.

The difference of one's true position in this world originates in race. This concept became clear to me when I was about 8 or 9 years old. I had a lot of childhood fantasies and dreams of becoming a fireman or a police officer. My brother Terry and I encountered two cops one day. I spoke to them about becoming a fireman or a police officer. The officer told me with malicious intent, "Nigger you are not going to become any of those things, it is not for your kind. I am going to take you to the pokey". So, I ran home and asked my mother what does that mean.

My mother told me it meant, "he is going to take you to jail". After that day, I no longer dreamed of being a fireman or police officer.

The officer shattered my dream. I believe being conscious of one's heritage and contributions to the past, present, and future, are the key to any one person being successful in their life. This defines my realization of being an African American in America.

Respectfully,

Delaney Franklin C-90255

Jonnie D

To whom that will read this, today's date is August 6, 2020. My name is Jonnie D. I am a half breed Apache Indian and Mexican. I was born in the year of 1958. I knew from a young age who I was because people seen I was different. Through the years people would not understand who I was because I did not look quite like a Mexican. I would let them know I was a half breed, and they would ask what that was. It was hard to tell them. I have gotten into some fights for who I am, but it did not change who I am. Those fights made me stronger in who I am if you can understand.

I remember one time I was in the checkout line at a store. Out of the corner of my eye I saw two older ladies looking at me. I knew they wanted to ask me by the way the shorter one kept pushing the taller one. When they finally came and asked me, the shorter one said to the taller one, "see I told you he was. I told you he was".

They just looked at me like they could not believe it. The look on their faces I can still see to this day. People look at you different when they don't know who you are. Many mistakes have been made because we all see things out of focus, when we need to open our eyes and minds, and look at people and their life through clear eyes. Then maybe through time and understanding we can help each other…. maybe?

Jonni D

Martin Hernandez

My name is Martin Hernandez I was born in the year of 1965. I am a Mexican American born in Mexico and raised in the United States. Part of my childhood was in Mexico, until the age of thirteen. In 1983, I migrated to the United States, not knowing how it was to live in another country.

In my first years as a new immigrant in the United States everything seemed to be joyful and peaceful. It was exciting to meet new people of different nationalities. To me this was an experience of a lifetime.

I was innocent of the barriers of race. I was learning that every nationality in the United States was different from my own. However, at the same time I seen everyone the same as a human being. In the years past something changed in me. I felt different seeing the world through a new lense. I noticed people from every culture, experiencing and demonstrating to others how proud they felt to be White, Black, Mexican and so on.

On my own understanding this was part of the United States culture, regardless of what nationality you come from. However, at the same time I seen everyone the same as being a human being.

States, culture, regardless of what nationality you come from, is the basis of how to live in a land. Based on my own experience, when my family found out about me going out with a girl, I remember my aunt asked me about who she was. My cousin was next to me, and he said, "es una guera!" which means it's a white girl. My aunt made a comment saying you should stick with your own. I ignored her and walked away saying to myself I really don't care. At the end I ended up getting married to her, regardless of what they thought. Now my kids are Mexican, and German born in the United States.

Darryl E

When Did I find out I was black?

I was born during the height of the civil rights movement in the year of 1962. A lot had already occurred that demonstrated the difference in who I was as a person. My parents were very protective of my siblings and I, as I grew up. Race and the color of my skin was not an issue that was talked about in my parents' house.

People of different races would visit our home a lot. Even in the ghetto, I had friends of different races that I would play with from time to time. By 1967 I realized that we were different than other's when my parents would take us on family trips down South to see our relatives. My father would give us very strict instructions on how to behave and when to move when he made stops on the way.

Plus, by that time I was able to watch television and from time to time I would see people that look like me and my family being terrorized by people of a different color, simply because of the color of their skin. This had never been talked about in my parent's home in front of us. I guess because my parents would shelter us from all of these things that were happening in the world.

Fast forward to 1974, this was my first encounter with racism. I was thirteen years of age; I was about two miles away from my home on my way to a friend's house. On this day, I was attacked by someone in the neighborhood just because I was black.

I was knocked off my bike and would have been beaten to death if I had not gotten way. That experience demonstrated to me what it means to be a black person in the United States of America. Even though I was attacked that day, strangely enough I still had a sense of pride. The racial taunts while being beaten didn't diminish my pride.

Later in my teens I realized that my skin color effected people when I was harassed by the police and then the gangs in my neighborhood. This happened often to me in school and later in work. From that time on the color of my skin seemed to determine everything about my life I became more and more angry.

My name is Darryl E. and I am a black man aka, an American of African descent.

Generation X

Late 60's- The 1970's

<u>Important Political Events:</u>

Watts's riots- 1967

Thurgood Marshall sworn in as first Black United States Supreme Court Justice- October 2, 1967

Roe v. Wade, Supreme Court ruled seven to two, January 22, 1973

President Nixon announce his resignation due to the Watergate scandal- august8, 1974

The Vietnam War ends- April 30, 1975

200th anniversary of the United States Independence- July 4, 1976

Sports

First Super Bowl in Los Angeles, Green Bay packers beat Kansas City Chiefs, 35 to 10-January 15, 1967

Wilt Chamberlain rookie of the year 1960; scouring leader- 1960,61,62,63,64,65,66 most valuable player 1960-1968; Points 31, 419; rebounds -23, 924

Olympic Swimmer Mark Spitz won seven gold medals in 1972- Munich, West Germany, August-September

Billie Jean King defeats Bobby Riggs in three straight set tennis match called "Battle of the sexes"- September 20, 1973, wins French Open -19782; Wimbledon 1966, 67, 68, 72, 73, 75

U.S. Open-1967, 1971-72, 1974; Australian Open- 1968

Reggie Jackson (Mr. October)- 1973 with 32 Home Runs 1975; M.V.P. 1973 MVP World Series 1973 36 bHome runs 1975 MVP World Series 1980 41 Home Runs 1980 Ten world Series Home Runs; 563 Home Runs

Jack Nicklaus- Masters 1963, 65, 66, 72, 75, 86; U.S. Open

1962, 67, 72, 80; British Open -1966, 70, 78, PGA 1963, 71, 73, 75, 80 Total Wins 18.

<u>Household Names</u>

The Beatles

Jimmy Hendricks

Whitey Bulger

Elvis Presley

Bill Cosby

<u>Popular Music</u>

Motown

Punk Rock

Classic Rock

R&B

Country

Funk

<u>Popular Television or Movies</u>

<u>Movies</u>

Star Wars

Jaws

Rocky

The Godfather I & II

<u>Television</u>

Brady Bunch

Good Times

Laugh Inn

Happy Days

Sandford & Son

American Bandstand

Soul Train

Wide World of Sports

The Midnight Special

<u>World Events</u>

Advanced Research Projects Agency (ARPA) of the United States Defense Department; ARPNET linked about 23 computers ("hosts ") at 15 sites, including Harvard and M.I.T.-1971

Reverend Dr. Martin Luther King, Jr. assassinated in Memphis, TN- April 4, 1968

Woodstock Rock Music Festival-Bethel, NY August 15-August 18, 1969

United States Astronauts: Neil Armstrong, Edwin "Buzz" Aldrin, and Michael Collins commanded "Apollo 11" to the moon; Armstrong was the first human being to set a foot on the moon.

President Nixon is the first United States president to visit Moscow; talks with the Kremlin in landmark strategic arms pact called "Salt I".

Jefferey A Garrett

When I found out I was black; By Jefferey A Garrett

Year of birth 1974

The date was September 12, 1979. My second week of elementary school, I attended El Sobrante Christian Elementary. It was made possible by one of my mothers' clients, as she was a hairdresser. My mother, siblings, and I lived in a middle-class neighborhood where there was a mix of different races. Everyone was either of Black, White, Hispanic, Asian, and Indian descent.

All the neighbors and their children were very cordial and friendly. They allowed their kids to play with all children in the neighborhood. Most of the children even spent nights at the other children's homes in the neighborhood over the weekends. So, my home life in no way prepared me for what I would encounter at school.

This new school I attended was very prestigious. You had to have money or know people, like my mother did with money, to gain admittance into this academic setting. I lived many miles away from the school, so my mother had to set up a carpool system so that I would make it to school daily on time.

My first week there was rough. Not knowing anyone, except the daughter of my mother's client who helped me, and my mother get in the school to have a chance at a better academic education. Upon day one of my new adventure, I noticed that 80 to 85 percent of the school was white the other 15 percent was mixed with Asian, Indian, and about two percent of Black American.

The daughter of my mother's client was White also, but she like many others in my neighborhood, had an infectious character and personality. I came to value this, while in my new unknown and unfamiliar environment. We both attended kindergarten AND were both in the same class, did recess together and lunch. After certain recess's there was this older group of white kinds who had to be three to five years older who would yell, "we're going to get you guys" and they would commence to chase us from the play area back to our classroom.

Shortly thereafter our mothers came to get us, the principle explained everything to them in its entirety. In the car I overheard our parents talking amongst each other and my friend's mother was saying to my mother the only reason this happened was because of my skin color.

At that moment I was confused. I was unsure of things, and I didn't know what to think. All I knew was that I didn't want that to happen again or any other type of madness that could conjure up fear. I loved everyone and that was all I knew; it was how I had been raised. Hearing my mother and her client (friend) speak to one another on the way back from school that day, I noticed how upset my mother's friend was of the fact those kids did those things to me and her daughter.

She screamed, cried, and cursed obscenities in the air. In a weird way it made me feel good inside although I had mixed feelings altogether.

When I finally reached home my mother and father spoke to each other about the incident at my school. My mom filled him in on the whole ordeal. I could hear him from behind my bedroom door saying how he didn't want me to go back there and how hateful and disrespectful those people were at the school; He raised his voice like he did on many occasions.

 He finally called me into the living room and asked me did I want to go back to the school and made me understand that it may happen again, I told him yes, I would go back. A couple days went by, and I was carpooled back to El Sobrante Christian were the first couple of days where good until the third day. On the third day, I experienced a similar form of fear from another group of individuals that wasn't physical but verbal and just as hurtful.

Shortly after, I was upset, hurt, angry, scared, and confused. I left that elementary school and was placed in a more open and racially mixed public school. From that experience, I noticed a change in my perspective about race. I became suspicious of people, guarded, and at times displayed anti-social behavior.

My new environment was the complete opposite of my previous elementary school, yet I found myself still the little boy with the girl who held my hand during recess and lunch. She was a beautiful soul who alerted me of the clear and present danger that would victimize me mentally and emotionally, altering my innocence as an adolescent.

A big percentage of my future encounters, with other human beings would be approached with caution, paranoia, and the uncertainty of the others motives and intentions. I would at some point; whether it was at the beginning, middle, or ending of the relation, take on the predatory role out of fear. I never wanted to experience the feeling that victimization caused.

People who loved and cared about me unconditionally were left confused, hurt, or angered by my brash and belligerent characteristics. This impeded my higher powers clear and tangible blessings. Hampering my healthy social interactions of greater human relations. They say, one's pain or shortcomings for the most part are self-inflicted, I believe this to be so.

I remember finding peace and happiness in recess and junior youth athletics. All through elementary school I excelled at tether ball and kick ball. I would take great pride in being the victor in tether ball during the full morning and afternoon recess.

During one recess, a group of white kids challenged me to several games of tether ball. The winner would receive cheers from the girl students, pats on the back from the fellows, and bragging rights. These challenges always placed my mind back to my experiences at El Sobrante Elementary.

These thoughts always helped me win the games. One by One I beat the four white kids with ease. Each game I would win at a four- or five-point advantage. These victories gave me a great sense of happiness, self-worth, and confidence. I would jump for joy while pumping my fist in the air yelling at them, "Y'all can't see me. I'm the best in the school."

Going into that contest with those kids, my frame of mind, motives, and intentions were wrong because when I first found out; it left me with a bias distain for White America. In that short time, I became that hate, that predator, searching for the prey. Being introduced and living in a form of social fear a defensive wall was built into my internal memory banks.

When in hindsight I should have thanked them for the challenge and possibly gave them tips on how acting in my ignorance. I continued in the universal disease that has been passed down and taught for generations. During my nurturance and insight on true love from my mother; I was already provided the knowledge of humility and the ideology of wanting for your brother what you want for yourself.

Fast forward to August 12, 2001, I arrived at High Desert State Prison, while getting processed I was informed about a nine-month lockdown that was imposed on all Black and Hispanic inmates due to a race riot on the yard, From there I was escorted with several other inmates of color to B-yard that housed all level four mainline inmates.

As I walked to my cell, my heartbeat fast as a race horse as the uncertainty overwhelmed me. The door to my cell slid open and I was greeted by a 6'2' 265-pound massive black man who wanted to know where my paperwork was. I complied with his every request. He then sat me down and explained to me what was happening at the prison. He told me that the Mexican Mafia (Southern Hispanics) stabbed Blacks on the yard killing two and seriously injuring the third.

Those acts set off a full-scale war between the Black and Hispanic races. He explained to me how the bad blood between the two races had been down South for many years now, and he said since I was born and raised up North I wouldn't understand. He went on to say I did need to understand that these Southern Hispanics didn't care where I was from. He said they wouldn't ask me where I was from, and that the only thing they saw was my skin color. He said all they knew was that I was a darker shade than them and that I needed to be killed with the rest of my kind when given the chance.

He then gave me what they called in prison a bone crusher, which was a six-to-eight-inch sharp jagged edge blade that would kill a lion. He then told me my older homie told him to give it to me so I could defend myself against an enemy I didn't know I had or didn't know existed. With fear, confusion and the clear and present thought of death I realized at that point that I was a Black man born and raised in North Richmond California, a Bay Area native all my life.

I was now faced with the highest form of fear I had ever experienced or dealt with in my life: racism.

R. Frost

There wasn't a signature moment in my life where I can now say with affirmed clarity in mind that defined when I absolutely became aware of my blackness. I will say that there were distinct moments in my early youth that were demonstrative and certainly instructional for me in regard to the dynamics of race in its interplay with virtually everything on this planet.

However, there was no single hometown for me in my youth, due to poverty (in principle) due to race. Thus, having moved around quite a bit in my youth (into cities of varying racial demographics) I had the rare luxury to experience my blackness early on through the eyes and lens of many different racial and ethnic perspectives. The differences of others were a mirror reflection of my difference.

I realize it has now become important to try to make note of those first moments of when someone first realized their Blackness. That seems worthwhile to positively awaken people's consciousness to their Blackness and the ongoing struggle that intertwines with it. However, I think it might be more important for all Black people, us as a people. to focus less on immutable aspects of our past, to instead concentrate on concrete solutions for creating a better future!

Respectfully,

R. Frost

Raymond Robledo Jr.

Date of Birth: June 6, 1975

Let me see; the first time I was called a racist name? I was about nine years old. In 1984, you know, the good ole days when you could run around the whole neighborhood and play with everyone. One day I was out playing, and some friends of mine (or so I thought), started calling me "Wetback" and "Beaner".

 I didn't know what those words meant. I know, I felt real bad inside, after I heard them, because the way they were said, were really mean. So, I went home and told my mom. I felt deep inside of my soul there was no reason for them to act like that. My mom sat me down and told me the history of my people (Indian/Mexican), and about racism. I didn't realize it then; but when I got older reality hit. It hurts my soul, because I know now that I can never recapture the joy of being a kid again.

Raymond Robledo, Jr.

Xavierre Sr.

Date of Birth: 1970

I found out, from a mental and physical standpoint; what it meant to be an American of African descent between the ages of six and twelve. My nurturer (Rose Jamison), my authority (Columbus Allen), and the Matriarch (Verneil Jamison) taught me to love all human beings. Not once at a department store, grocery store or the church did they ever comment or visually display hate, or disregard for any human being.

When I was ten years old my Matriarch sat me down and read the Bible to me, as she always did. I distinctively remember this moment and the scripture. She read Matthew 10:40-42. In this passage 'Water' is nurturance and over the years these words have instilled physical and emotional care. Moments later, we watched the movie *Roots*. The movie was horrifying to me.

Watching White men hunt Kunta Kenta like a dog created an internal fear of "a White man" in my soul. But when they caught him, and chopped off his foot, it heightened my fear to terror. Nevertheless, this was my first internal introduction to hate-by watching human brutality.

A couple of years later my Uncle Willie got out of jail. His aura was gigantic like a Nephilim. I took to his nature. Frequently, me and Uncle Willie would walk to the liquor store. One time on our way back from the liquor store, I said, "Hey Unk, I want a job".

He said, "Okay, go knock on that building's (he pointed to the first red brick building), front door, and ask them do they have any job openings?"

I walked up to the door and knocked. Seconds later, a White man came to the door and said "What can I do for you son?"

In FEAR, I looked back at Uncle Willie for assurance; he smiled and nodded his head. I turned back around slightly relaxed and said, "Sir do you have any job openings?"

He looked at my uncle with a slight smile and nodded. He stuck out an open hand, and said, "my name is Julie, and this is my furniture factory."

I slowly shook his hand. He then stated, "Yes, young man. You can work here the whole summer; Monday through Friday, from three o'clock to five o'clock for $25 a week, cleaning the office and the break room."

I gave him a big Kool-aid smile, and said, "Thank you sir." I quickly walked over to Uncle Willie, and said, "That man said I can work the whole summer for $25.00 a week. Unk, what is a break room?"

"It's a room you eat in at work, and Zay make sure you do a good job."

I smiled and started eating my Boston Bake Beans; Uncle Willie bought me at the liquor store.

A few weeks later; working at the furniture factory, one of the guys in the office said, "Hey little nigger boy!" I kept working; I didn't know what that meant my name was Xavierre. He walked up to me and snatched the broom out of my hands.

He yelled, "Little nigger boy-you heard me talking to you."

I remember being scared to death as this big White man towered over me. In terror, I said nothing. Julie entered the room, quickly walked up, and stood between me and the big man. Facing the big man, Julie said, "you stupid piece of shit, that's a kid. Get your shit and get the fuck out of my building, you're fired!" Julie turned to me and said, "I'm sorry Xavierre. Don't ever let no one call you that word."

He stuck his hand out again. I paused but shook his hand. He went into his pocket and pulled out twenty dollars and handed it to me. I took the money and smiled. I Years later, went back to thank Julie's, but the furniture factory was gone.

Therefore, years later, soaked by the act of hate, my apparent arrested development embraced a guise of a pseudo intellectual. I then attended to a parasitic behavior. As a drug dealer, my next stop was prison. Being thrust into the cesspool of dog eat dog, this microcosm demanded tribalism.

The structural oversight of violent leaders would weed out the weak and abuse those who don't know any better. In this environment, racial supremacy institutes a diabolical nature that's sought after. The segregated policies mirrored the 'separate' but equal doctrine of Plessy V. Ferguson of 1896.

I can recall working in the prisons kitchen where the policies of segregation descend all the way down to a pack of peanut butter and the monetary value of a slice of bread.

On occasion, the distribution of coffee grounds seemed to be unfair to a member of the 'La Raza', (a phrase used by Mexicans to denote 'Mestizo', (Spanish and Native American ethnic mix ancestry), with the spokesperson not working that day; an overly zealous individual name Sammy, took it upon himself to speak on behalf of the 'Laraza', in the kitchen.

In a previous villainous thought; knowing the one is out of rank, and seeks individual power-becomes Bart. This manufactured belief of inherently ethnic superiority to assist this pond to masquerade as a knight displays a prison tactic of racial deception. The exultation is to eliminate a few of ones' opponents. When the 'LaRaza' became aware of the rule change, which was outside of their approval, they were furious. Their spokesperson even attempted to renegotiate for the original agreement to be reinstated.

Recognizing a chink in their armor, they were informed, "absolutely not", knowing the response will enact an immediate reaction for disciplinarily measures. Sammy quickly came to me and asked if I could help him by speaking with the "Brothers", (Blacks) to undo the coffee deal.

With no remorse, I told Sammy, "Dog you knew the job was dangerous when you took it."

Sammy pleaded with me, describing the shame that will ensure if he couldn't correct this mistake. Knowing I could have helped him; I continued to refuse to, due to my ignorance, and fear of being ostracized. In my conscious state of disregard, I contemplated it was more important to see the 'Laraza' assault their own, then to save the integrity of Sammy.

How dare I not recognize and attend to the internal terror I know so well. I was responsible to administer a similar form of nurturance, just as I received in the mist of dismay. Sammy, please forgive me for not being empathetic to your emotional needs.

During my previous state of deviance, I fueled toxic thoughts to my underdeveloped cerebrum. This made way for my engrams, (painful, negative mental images representing a past event), to identify as reality. Because of acts of such callousness, I'm fully committed to taking on a lifelong campaign of social amends to humanity.

Julie, if you, or someone who knows him reads this, please tell him thank you for being a decent human being, and a catalyst at the beginning of my understanding, which was pivotal to what true 'Altruism' looks like.

Generation Y

1980s-Late 1990s

Important Political Events:

52 American hostages in Iran were freed after being held, August 16, 1981

President Reagan was shot in Washington D.C. March 30, 1981

United States Centers for Disease Control reports first cases of what became known as 'A.I.D.S' June 5, 1981

The United States Senate confirmed the appointment of first female Supreme Court Justice, Sandra Day O'Connor September 21, 1981

Harold Washington (democrat) elected first black mayor of Chicago IL, April 12, 1983

Space shuttle 'Challenger' launch from Cape Canaveral Florida June 18, 1983, carrying the first American woman Sally Ride into space.

Geraldine Ferraro (Democrat, New York), became the first woman nominated as Vice Presidential candidate. June 6, 1984

Space shuttle 'Challenger' explodes 73 seconds after liftoff, January 28 1986

Iran –Contra affair is heard by Senate and House Committee May 5, 1987

A.Z.T. first drug shown to be effective in the fight against A.I.D.S. is approved by F.D.A., March 20, 1987

Surgeon General, C. Everett Koop declared cigarettes addictive May 16, 1988

Army General Colin Powell became first black Chairman of Joint Chiefs of Staff under President George H. W. Bush, August 10, 1989

The World Trade Center's underground parking lot is bombed in New York City, February 26, 1993

'Don't ask, don't tell' policy for homosexuals in the military was announced by President Clinton, July 19, 1993

Truck bomb exploded outside Oklahoma City Federal Office April 19, 1995

'Million Man March' in Washington D.C. October 16, 1995

<u>Sports</u>

Martina Navratilova tennis champion at Australian Open, 1981, 1983, 1985

French Open 1982, 1984; Wimbledon 1978, 1979, 1982, 1983, 1984, 1985, 1986, 1987, 1990; U.S. Open 1983, 1984, 1986, 1987

Mike 'Iron Man' Tyson becomes the youngest undisputed Heavyweight Champion WBA, WBC, IBF) August 1, 1987 in Las Vegas

Michael Jordan Rockie of The Year 1985; Scoring Leader 1987, 1988, 1989, 1990, 1991, 1992, 1993, 1996, 1997, 1998; M.V.P. in NBA Finals 1991, 1992, 1993, 1996, 1997, 1998; Defensive Player of the Year 1988; Points 32, 292; Field Goals Made 12, 192; steals 2, 514; NBA Finals Championships Title with the Chicago Bulls, 6 Titles

San Francisco 49ers Super Bowl Winners 1982, 1985, 1989, 1990, 1995

Buffalo Bills Super Bowl Loses 1991, 1992, 1993, 1994

United States wins Olympic Gold over U.S.S.R. in Sweden 1980;

Roger Clemons played for 4 MLB Teams; M.V.P. 1986; Cy Young Award 1986, 87, 91, 97, 98, 2001, 2004; Strikeouts 1988:291, 1991:241, 1996:257, 1997:292. 1998:271; Victory Leaders by season 1986:24, 1987:20, 1997:21, 1998:21; All time MLB Strikeouts 4,672; Pitchers with 300 MLB wins 354; Earned Run Average Leaders by Season 1986 G:33, IP:2540, ERA:2.48; 1990 G:31 IP:228.1, ERA:1.93, 1991 G:35, IP:271.1 ERA:1.93, 1992 G:32, IP:246.2, ERA:2.41, 1997 G:34, IP:264.o, Era 12.05, 1998 G:33, IP:234.2, ERA:2.65

<u>Household Names</u>

Madeline Albright

Manual Noriega

Pete Rose

RUN DMC

Sugar Ray Leonard

O.J. Simpson

<u>Popular Music</u>

New Wave

Reggae

Heavy Rock

R&B

Rhythm & Poetry (R.A.P.)

Pop Music

Grunge

<u>Popular Television Shows or Movies</u>

Officer and a Gentleman

Silence of the Lambs

Forrest Gump

Boyz N The Hood

Braveheart

Titanic

Television Shows:

The Cosby Show

Cheers

Murphy Brown

N.Y.P.D. Blue

Frasier

Hill Street Blues

L.A. Law

Seinfeld

Fresh Prince of Bel Air

World Events:

John Lennon (of the Beatles) was killed December 8, 1980, in New York City.

Michael Jackson's Thriller Album released November 30, 1982

Persian Gulf war ends February 27, 1991

North American Free Trade Agreement (NAFTA)January 1, 1994

The Columbine High School Shooting April 20, 1999

A.K.A. Moe

Author- A.K.A. Moe

Date of Birth: 1992

When I was a young kid, I was in the system. I went from group home to group home. At these programs most of the staff was African American. So being a kid without any parental figures in my life, I started to adopt the 'swagger' traits of the lifestyle, and the community portrayed by the African Americans. Mind you; my skin color is brown.

The heritage or swagger of my ethnicity (Mexican) was not of the nature I adopted. So being raised the way I chose, was because of the opportunity of being able to fit in with what society called an outcast. So, with that I felt I was an outcast too.

As time moved on and I got older, I had to "step in line" so to speak, because of my family associations and skin color. I had to become something I truly despised. I was becoming the kind of person that has to follow rules, guidelines, and bad intentions toward people, society and anyone who was not of Mexican descent.

If your mixed, but your Hispanic side is dominate, then you were good. Letting someone else beliefs dictate my actions was disheartening as I look back. But knowing what I know now; I can be clearer about me, myself, and I. Please believe I love and care about the value of all human life as it is, and not the color our skin is.

Michael James Goree

Year of Birth: 1979

When I Found Out:

I was 11 years old when I started looking at the same sex. But I never said anything to anyone because I grew up in a Christian home and being black and bisexual is taboo. So, I kept it to myself for years. But once I got older and became more confident in myself and no longer cared what people said, I started coming out more to people like me.

Just a few years ago I came out to my mother, the one that I'm closest to. She didn't accept my lifestyle. But the one I thought was going to be the hardest was my father. He accepted my lifestyle. My life is better now that I've came out and I don't need to hide anymore about who I am. Some people can accept it and some people can't and I'm okay with that. For those that accept my lifestyle, thank you! And for those that don't, I thank you also!

Michael James Goree

Gerald

Year of Birth: 1982

When I Found Out:

I can remember from an early age the bigoted things my dad said. My mom always disapproved of him saying such things in front of my brother and me. I had no frame of reference for a whole class of people accepting what I saw on television and what my parents said. I also remember the ignorance that I took part in with my friends as a kid. We would call each other names and play games which promoted violence against people who were different.

I was in the sixth grade, eleven years old when I was bullied by other students. I was awkward with girls, and I was already ashamed of myself. The very first time I remember the urge I was riding the yellow bus to school.

I saw a construction worker with his shirt off. I instantly felt an attraction to the construction worker. I was instantly afraid. I was the "fruit loop" my dad had been making jokes about. I was the "fag", the dirtiest insult that didn't involve "your mom". I was the "queer" that got "smeared" in our version of tackle tag with footballs.

I was instantly afraid. What if someone could tell? Maybe that was why I was always picked last for every pickup game. Maybe that was why girls didn't like me. Maybe that was why I was so unpopular. Maybe that was why my dad didn't love me.

I don't know how well I was hiding it before I knew. After all, I wasn't trying to hide it at all. After I found out, I hid it so well that I hid it from myself. My denial was not total; I had occasion to be reminded of my secret shame. This was not a frequent occurrence, and I quickly managed to forget a part of myself.

Overcompensation, in my case, only lasted a little while. By the time my peers were sophisticated enough to distinguish it, the "secretly gay tough guy" was a cliché, and my mask was machismo with tolerance for gays.

The mask slipped occasionally, but I could not get over the shame until I let go of it willingly and started being myself.

I still have some fear.

Gerald

Vincent H.

Year of Birth: 1983

There are seasons in life when one has an "aha moment". During those periods in those seasons, one comes to realizations and becomes enlightened. Not only does one become educated, one also can become empowered. Both have benefits beyond comprehension. With that being said, I'm not exempt.

I found out that I was Black during the month of September. The year was 1989 and I was entering the front doors of Brandywood Elementary school. I entered my first-grade homeroom class and I noticed that the other students looked alike, and none looked like me. Most of them distanced themselves from me. One White student sat next to me and introduced himself to me.

"Hi, my name is Michael. What's your name?"

I responded immediately, "My name is Vincent."

Later on that day, I asked Michael, "How come nobody wants to be my friend?"

With level honesty, Michael replied, "Because you're Black." That's when I found out I was Black. Two weeks later, I decided to introduce myself to a few of my classmates during recess. As most children are at recess, some are in different circles, running around, laughing, playing and what not.

I walked up to a few of my male peers to introduce myself.

"Hi, I'm Vincent, can I play with y'all?"

They laughed in unison and began to joke about my skin color. Then one boy picked up rocks, threw them at me and his friends joined in as well. I was frightened and ran away as fast as I could.

I caught up with Michael and told him what happened. Then he told me how they were jerks and said that he would introduce me to some of his friends. For me, reality kicked in that my skin color was responsible for me feeling out of place, almost like an outsider looking in. I ended up making a few more friends after that, and sometimes I felt like that made things better.

For example, on February 14, 1990, every student in the classroom had a Valentine's bag. The difference between everyone else's bags and mine was that theirs had candy and cards in them. Mines were completely empty. I was devastated and since that day, I never celebrated Valentine's Day.

Part 2:

No lie can live forever…

On April 2018, I was arrested for trespassing on a Drexel University Fraternity Property. The lead officer asked me "What are you doing here?"

I responded. What the officer told me next struck a nerve, which almost paralyzed me permanently. "You're too old for College, so don't even waste your time. You are under arrest, and you have the right to remain silent."

Two weeks later, the judge dismissed my case. Two and a half years later, I'm about to become a free man and intend to further my education, majoring in Creative Writing and proving to myself that the lies I once believed are dead, buried and will never resurface again, What lives from this point forward is taking place in the facts that:

1. It's never too late to acquire higher learning and

2. Education is never a waste of time...

No lie can live forever!!!!

Vincent

Generation Z

(Millennials)

Late 1990-2020

<u>Important Political Events:</u>

Same sex couples Vermont gained the legal rights to form 'civil unions' with signed legislation in April 26, 2000:

The FDA ANNOUNCED, AND APPROVAL OF 'RU-486': a pill that induces abortions September 28, 2000

President Bush creates 'Office of Homeland Security' on October 8, and on October 26, signed 'Patriot Act' to prevent terrorism-2001

'D.C. Sniper', John Mohammad is found guilty by a Virginia jury in Washington D.C. November 17, 2002:

Massachusetts becomes the first U.S. State where 'Same Sex Marriage Legal 2004

Alberto Gonzales became first Hispanic U.S. Attorney General under President George Walker Bush 2005

<u>Sports</u>

Boston Red Sox won World Series for the first time since October 27, 2004

Tiger Woods Masters winnings: 1997, 2001, 2002, 2005, 2018; Us Open 2000, 2002, 2008, ; Britain Open 2000,

2005, 2006; PGA: 1999, 2000, 2006, 2007; Fed Ex Cup: 2007, 2009

Floyd Mayweather Jr. Welterweight WBC Champion: 2006, 2007, 2008, 2011, 2012, 2013, 2014, 2015, 2016, 2017, 2018; Lightweight Champion: 2002, 2003, 2004; Super Welterweight-----; 50 wins, No losses

New England Patriots Super Bowl Winners: 2002, 2004, 2005, 2015, 2017, 2019:

Usain Bolt Olympic 100 Meter Gold medal Winners: 22008, 2012, 2016; 200 meter Gold Medal Winners: 2008, 2012, 2016; 100 meter record:9.58 seconds, August 16, 2009; 200 Meter Record 19.19 Seconds August 20, 2009; 400 meter(4x100) 36. 84 seconds, August 11, 2012

Michael Phelps Olympic Swimmer 200 Meter Free-Style, 2008; 100 meter butterfly: 2004, 2008, 2012; 200 Meter Butterfly, 2004, 2008; 100 meter individual medley, 29004, 2008, 2012; 400 Meter Individual Medley: 2004, 2008

Tom Brady Super Bowl wins 2002, 2004, 2005; Super Bowl M.V.P. 2002, 2004, 2007, 2010

Lebron James NBA 1st round draft pick;, 2003; Rookie of the year 2004, Finals M.V.P. 2012, 2013, 2017; All Time Scoring GP:842, Pts: 23, 173, Avg:27.5; Finals Appearances 2007(loss) 2011(loss) 2012 (win) 2013 (win) 2014 (loss) 2015(loss) 2016 (loss) 2017(win)

Team of the Generation San Antonio Spurs with five NBA Title Finals Victories 1999, 2003, 2005, 2007, 2014; with

Gregg Popovich as Head Coach who was Coach of the year 2003, 2012, 2014

<u>Household Names:</u>

Oprah Winfrey

Steve Jobs

Dr. Fauci

Steve Jobs

Donald Trump

Barack Obama

Edward Snowden

Beyonce

Osama Bin Laden

Jay Z

El Chapo

Popular Music:

Hip-Hop

BKA-R.A.P.

Pop Music

Country

Reggaeton

<u>Popular Television or Movies:</u>

<u>Movies</u>

Guardians of the Galaxy

The Lord of the Rings

The Return of the King

Fast & the Furious

Million Dollar Baby

No Country for Old Men

12 Years of a Slave

The Artist

Television Shows

Friends

Modern Family

Survivor

Empire

Mad Men

American Idol

<u>World Events</u>

Saddam Hussein captured and later hung to death 2003

President Bush confirms the existence of secret overseas prisons ran by the C.I.A. September 6, 2006

Iraq War March 19, 2003-December 15, 2011

Facebook the social media giant initial public offering (stock exchange) raised 16 billion May 18, 2012

Michael Jackson dies

Occupy Wall Street expands across the United States and overseas

Isaiah A.

Year of Birth 1996

The day I realized my skin color:

When I was about thirteen years old, I remember my older sister Joanna, she was two and half years older than me, expressed herself. It was me she expressed herself to. Joanna explained to me and my mother that she had experienced a raciest act directed toward her.

It was difficult for me to image what that would have been like for her or me because the lifestyle I was living was much different. I would say about six months later I experienced a similar event. A car raced down my block as multiple individuals in it yelled out the vehicle at me, "Hey Nigger."

I challenged them to stop. To get out of the car and face me because that's the type of lifestyle I was living. I never had that experience in my hometown again. But from that time on I was aware and gained knowledge about racism. I was also taught to stick up for myself in many more ways than one but to do so regardless of the situation eight to ten times.

Over time you gain a sense of when to stand and when to walk away. The color of one's skin with the way people talk or if their right-handed or left. We are people. We are human and I'm not racist toward people.

Ade H.

Date of Birth: 7/4/1999

When I was a kid, maybe six or seven my teacher called my mom and told her I had been misbehaving in class. I knew I was going to get in trouble, but I did not know that her scolding would be more about the color of my skin.

When I got home my mom was furious. She told me that I was African American; (Black). She said anything I do would always be five times worse than anything a White person or Latin person does. I understood exactly what she meant. However, I did not understand why it had to be that way.

From that moment on I always looked for things to confirm what my mother said. I would come home and tell her stories and ask her if the person was racist. Growing up in San Jose California, where African Americans are only three percent of the population, this happened often.

In fifth grade a Mexican boy, around my age called me nigger on the school bus. I threatened to hit him, and he did not say anything else. Years later, in ninth grade, I was living in Reno, Nevada. I had only been there for two weeks when walking home and four older White high schoolboy's called me a nigger as they drove by in a forest green SUV.

Seth A.

Year of Birth: 1998

My name is Seth. I was born in 1998 and grew up back and forth between the Central Valley and the Bay Area. I am Caucasian and I have always known that I was White, but the moment I officially realized I was different from the other men my age is when I was eighteen years old and went to County Jail for the first time.

My family is far from racist, I was raised to see people not by their skin color but by their heart and character. Growing up my friends were from every ethnological background, and I distanced myself from anybody that judged people by their heritage. In 2016, I got booked into Tulare County Jail for possession of a firearm and felony evading.

My first day I was approached by a few inked up White guys, and they asked me if I was a "White boy". I felt it was a dumb question due to my obviously white skin and blue eyes, but I said yes regardless and we shook hands and parted ways.

Later that day I ran into one of my good friends named Tray and he was African American. We were happy to see each other, and he made me a burrito. The White guy's seen that I was eating with a "Black" and ran in and it turned into a small race riot, some people were seriously injured.

Once the police broke us up, we all went to the hole and that's when I realized I was actually different from other men around me. To this day I judge people off their actions not color. I am going to raise my children that way as well. I believe the world would be a much more beautiful place if more people lived that way.

#All Lives Matter

Little John

Year of Birth: 1995

It started in Fresno California, in the summer of July 11, 1995, when a young king was born by the name Calvin Charles Little John. My father, aka, Calvin Little John II was a drug dealer. He wasn't a bad father he just wanted to keep the lights on and food on the table.

My mother aka, Wahna Little John was sweet Lil Asian lady, who was solid as a brick. She stood by her husband right or wrong. This story is about when I learned about racism.

The year was 2001. I was six, when I saw the police beat my dad because they said he sold drugs. After the beatings they still took him to jail for almost four years. The crazy part about it was the Black cops who took part in the beating, confused the hell out of me; for the officers were the same color as us.

Then I started thinking about my Cousin Malcolm, my pops best cuddy. He's in prison for 44 years to life for a crime they said he committed, but that he did not get caught for. But a witness said that it looked like him, but he wasn't sure.

It was my cousin's past criminal history, that's all the judge needed to hear. I was four years old at that time and I remember my dad was like (evil) racists asses. But I didn't know what he was talking about. But now that I am older I see, that it's just not Whites, Mexicans or Asians that are racists.

I am in a gang and there's so much black on black crime it's crazy that I lost brothers and cousins to my own kind. Now, I am like forget the world its family over everything.

Tayari P.

Year of Birth 2000

When I first found out:

I was born in a little city in Northern California in the year 2000. Until the age of five, my memories consisted mostly of going back and forth between my mother and father's house. Until one day, when one of my mom's many boyfriends beat me.

 My father soon after took full custody of me. My dad decided we were moving to Hawaii in 2005. Up to this point I had never interacted with kids that were not White.

After a few days of settling into our new home, it was now time to get enrolled at my new school.

The first day of school I noticed instantly how different life was going to be. Besides me there was only two other White kids in school, within my first week I encountered racism. To explain the kids would refer to me as "Halle". Which I later learned is what Hawaiians called White people who were not locals on the island.

The abuse would vary from teasing and being made an outcast to on some occasions getting into fights. As this went on for two years or so over my own color or where I came from completely stopped. For instance, there were kids that even after four to five years going to school with them never saw me as anything but a "Halle".

All in all, it took understanding where racism stems from to overcome it. Which I believe come from ignorance.

Conclusion

The intercultural difference amongst those of the same genetic background, sometimes pose social friction. Meanwhile, the lack of willful understanding in relation to those who are genetically different magnifies the friction.

This friction revolves around the competitive component of human beliefs, values, customs, and habits, where one will quickly assassinate the character of the other human being. By way of ignorance, the abusive nature builds a cerebral case of bias, and fictitious evidence. During this social confusion, the one who is willing to utilize this behavior, is hell bent on villainizing the other human being to gain social traction.

This debasement (lowering of character) becomes a mental reward, thus re-enforcing the continuous pursuit to quench the abusive thirst.

What is not intellectually understood; is that this is a self-exposure of hatred of self. The corruptness of man is the result of one's adopted abusive nature, because of the constant pursuit of gratifying self by reason of ignorance. This mind state disregards the proper usage and meaning of practical wisdom within a moral choice.

The lack of therapy, in relation to virtues-enacts the innate tendency to destroy. In reference to what's practical and reasonable, is being able to consciously decipher the essence of a moral choice. This is done by identifying and acknowledging a point of judicious obligation to oneself.

An academic recognition is conjured with reasoning, truth, displaying human goodness for others or a situation, and APT (suitable or appropriate) to do what's pleasing to other human beings.

APT (suitable or appropriate) to do what's pleasing to other human beings. Let's be seated in a universal perspective. For clarity, this is a nation of immigrants with many customs, beliefs, and values. In relation to our nation's constitution, its intention-is to provide the resources for all civilians to adjust and confirm as citizens of this sovereign nation.

Within that sovereignty; there's a course of individuality. The plight of our nation is the systematic recitation of a series of events. The events continue to address the content of a topic manifesting into an abusive platitude. Just as one would, or might say, "his unfortunate what happen, but that's how it is."

So in exchange, 'when did you find out' becomes a vehicle in assisting our nation to identify the opportunity to communicate, debate, or discuss a new narrative. This will unveil the society within each of us allowing this nation to embrace universality.

Suggested Readings

The Equilibrium Program:

This self-help program unveils the unique social skills of human compatibility; by using a formula an algorithm to expose the similarities, and preference-that we all have in common.

Author: Xavierre Allen Sr.

Emotional Preference:

This handbook/Self Help program utilizes 'Four subject matters': Emotional Builders, Emotional Pivot, Emotional Resiliencies, and sustained emotions. Each subject matter host a lesson plan which chips away at generational ignorance. There's an academic examination of how the cerebral hemisphere relates to ones thought process; its introduction to preference, and the tools to decipher for emotional stability.

Author Xavierre Allen Sr.

H.O.O.D (Helping. Others. Optimize. Development)

This handbook has a complete self-help program within it. H.O.O.D, first introduces 'Cause' by using reverse engineering techniques to identify the disturbing patterns of a behavior. Next, is 'Diagnosis'; which utilizes the Diagnostic statistical manual of mental Disorder-Iv-Text Revision (DSM-IV-TR)by incorporating its five separate 'Axis'. Then there's 'Treatment' it's focused around two parts: 1. Cognitive psychology and Restructuring 2.

Virtues. Finally; there's a realistic 'Clinical Picture' allowing the testimonies of real people to establish a template.

Xavierre Allen Sr. Brandon Burris, Phillip Norris

For more information contact:

Xavierre_Allen@icloud.com

References

Anthropologist Ashley Montagu-author of "The Concept of Race"; New York: Free Press, 1964; and "Face and I.Q.": Expanded Edition, new York: Oxford University Press, 1999

Sociologist James M. Henslin-author of, "A Down-To Earth Approach, Seventh Edition: Refer to Pages 234; 324; 327.

Wikitionary based Endictionary created:

Thru January 3, 2013. 14:22:14

'College Writing Skill With Readings' sixth edition, author John Langan. P.566-569(proper nouns)

INDEX

Xavierre Allen Sr.

Hello human race, this is my Epitome of life. During my years of deviancy, I entertained an abusive nature, creating a vindictive spirit. By reason of ignorance, I socially and emotionally bullied those I encountered with an aggressive demeanor.

I assumed the coolness of a villain was the emotional accolades I yearned for. This social destitute placed me in the crosshairs where my son, Xavierre Jr., wrote me a letter enclosed with a profound question. He said, "Dad if you love me so much why you didn't stop doing what you were doing when I was born?"

This knife of exposure divulged an emotional rock bottom to my consciousness. I made a commitment to advance beyond my limits of elementary studies. I addressed my arrested development, aptitude, and patterns of functioning as a mental patient. I am now conscious of my own ignorance.

I will no longer assassinate my character and never again auction off my soul for material things. After successfully obtaining my degree in Business from Coastline Community College, I went on a verbal campaign.

During this campaign, I expressed an identity to my accomplishment by using the 'paper degree' as a form of boosting my character with no tangible substance. This vacancy created a void, and I felt like a paper champion. The overwhelming urge to achieve something of substance become the method of capturing the restoration of my character.

At this moment, my understanding provided the most valuable source of growth concerning the changing of my product (my core interest) from illegal to legal. I also identified the importance of extracting the useful attributes that will stimulate the unwavering commitment furnished by a desirous ambition.

So I embarked on a rigorous journey of auto-didactic. Meeting the other authors was approached with sure precautionary measures. I know it's in my best interest, socially, to befriend all human beings. Not being 'privy' to Mr. Garrett's or Mr. Eberhard's emotional position concerning our nation's pre-prescribe identification in relation to 'Race', I took precautions.

 It was imperative of me to be willing to accept their perspective concerning 'pigmentocracy'. We engaged in deep and reflecting dialogues back to the source of what we conclude is our nation root to deception. This established the birth of *When did You Find Out*.

J. Garrett

I Jeffery Garrett, arrived back to Valley State Prison, the institution, which caused me and my family displeasure and stress. During my entrance, I was under harsh scrutiny, which led to my mental confusion. I contemplated, "make the best out of a bad situation". Shortly thereafter, it was revealed to me that, "you were brought back here for a real reason and purpose".

At that time, to me any reason or purpose was crazy and farfetched. However, the person who spoke those words to me held a spiritual space in my soul. I respected, admired, and valued her opinion as if it was the Gospel. I spent the next month exercising vigorously. This kept my mind free of any negative thoughts or engaging in baseless conversation with others that held no value. Meanwhile, I noticed my soul and spirit was yearning for a change. A spiritual awakening and enlightenment I wasn't receiving from exercising.

I prayed and meditated long for a spiritual awakening to manifest. One morning, before my daily routine of exercising; me and my workout buddy, Demarie were on our way outside. Suddenly, I heard a voice, "Aye Demarie".

I looked over and noticed a human being, who I didn't know. We walked over to him and Demarie introduced me to Mr. Allen. Upon our initial encounter with Mr. Allen, I noticed humbleness, and positive aura encompassed him. He then verbally discussed a plethora of self help, awareness, and social unity principles. He also passed documents for us to read in relation to the curriculum he created for the youth inside prison and in the community. At that moment, I felt a glimpse of the enlightenment and awakening I whole heartedly desired.

My thirst of judicious ambition was quenched. Mr. Allen and I spoke in-depth about our life experience and how we together will make a positive impact by making amend, living up to our God given purpose, and work on our legacy.

If one could be reunited with their inter-self. Would you do it? So Uncovering the truth concerning the ascribed status. Will grant you the freedom to choice. WHEN DID YOU FIND OUT? allows that nurturance to proclaim its natural place is our society.

A multicultural group of incarcerated men, from various ethnicities, sexual preferences, and different ages tell the stories of when they found out their pre-prescribed race. It's a psychological picture of how these men not only come to learn their identity, but also formulate how they would interact with others. These men all show that one is not born a racist. It is a learned behavior. Not only are racist acts hurtful, but they also change the course of humanity.

J. Eberhard

Mr. Eberhard has been released and is currently working on reestablishing himself as a valued member of society. He is very passionate about the When Did You Find Out project and is currently working to help promote the book from the 'outside'.